Geography Starts

VOLCANOES

Claire Llewellyn

Heinemann Library
Chicago, Illinois

Published by Heinemann Interactive Library,
an imprint of Reed Educational & Professional Publishing,
Chicago, IL

Customer Service 888-454-2279

Visit our website at www.heinemannlibrary.com

Designed by David Oakley
Illustrations by Hardlines (p. 7) and Jo Brooker
Printed in China

08 07
10 9 8 7 6 5

Library of Congress Cataloging-in-Publication Data
Llewellyn, Claire.
    Volcanoes/ Claire Llewellyn.
        p. cm. – (Geography starts)
    Includes bibliographical references and index.
    Summary: An introduction to volcanoes and how they work, describing their formation,
destructive forces, and benefits.
        ISBN 1-57572-207-0 (lib. bdg.)   ISBN 1-58810-979-8 (pbk. bdg.)
        ISBN 978-1-57572-207-8 (lib.bdg.)   ISBN 978-1-58810-979-8 (pbk.bdg.)
        1. Volcanoes—Juvenile literature. [1. Volcanoes.] I. Title. II. Llewellyn, Claire.
Geography starts.

    QE521.3.L58 2000
    551.21—dc21   99-051656

Acknowledgments
The Publishers would like to thank the following for permission to reproduce photographs:
Colorific!/Baron Sakiya, p. 12; FLPA/A. A. Riley, p. 5; FLPA/A. Nardi/Panda Photo, p. 26; FLPA/USGS, p. 6; FLPA/USDA
Forest Service, p. 13; FLPA/S. Jonasson, p. 14; FLPA/R. Holcomb, p. 18; FLPA/Jurgen & Christine Sohns, p. 20;
NASA/Johnson Space Center, pp. 22, 24; Oxford Scientific Films/Survival Anglia/Joan Root, p. 4; Oxford Scientific
Films/Frank Huber, p. 10; Oxford Scientific Films/David B. Fleetham, p. 15; Robert Harding Picture Library/Adina Tovy,
p .8; Robert Harding Picture Library/A. C. Waltham, p. 9; Robert Harding Picture Library/Kim Hart, p. 19; Robert
Harding Picture Library/Tony Waltham, p. 21; Science Photo Library/NASA, p. 11; Still Pictures/Reinhard Janke, p. 16;
Still Pictures/John Cancalosi, p. 17; Trip, p. 29; Trip/P. Nicholas, p. 28.

Cover photograph reproduced with permission of Robert Harding Picture Library.

Some words are shown in bold, **like this**. You can find
out what they mean by looking in the glossary.

Contents

What Is a Volcano?

A volcano is an opening in the earth's surface. In its center is a hole that goes down into the middle of the earth. When the volcano **erupts**, it shoots out red-hot liquid rock.

A stream of liquid rock pours out of a volcano.

When the hot rock comes out of the volcano, it is called **lava**. The lava then cools and hardens. This slowly builds the volcano up into a mountain. It may be years before the volcano erupts again.

The sides of this volcano are made of solid lava.

What Starts a Volcano?

The earth is made of rock. On the surface of the earth, the rock is cool and hard. Underneath, the rock is hot and liquid. This liquid rock is called magma while it is in the earth.

A **gas** in magma makes it burst out of the earth.

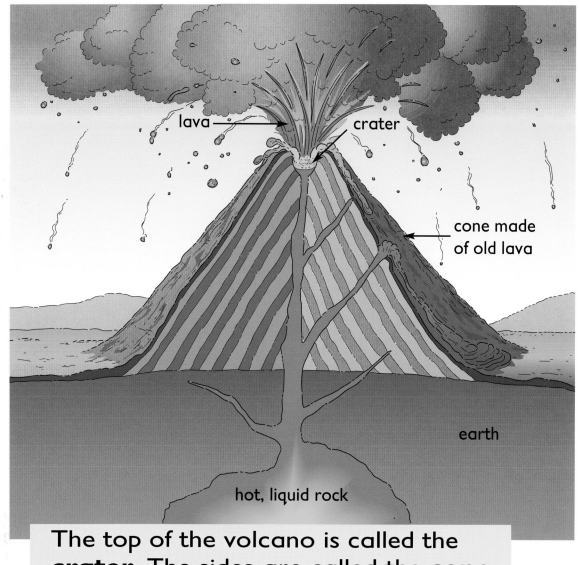

lava — crater

cone made of old lava

earth

hot, liquid rock

The top of the volcano is called the **crater**. The sides are called the **cone**.

A volcano is like a chimney with a large opening at the top. The magma is pushed up the chimney. When the volcano erupts, magma from inside the earth comes out of the top. Then it is called **lava.**

Building a Volcano

Mount Fuji in Japan has very steep sides.

Sometimes, the **lava** is so thick that it runs downhill very slowly. As it hardens, it builds a mountain with very steep sides.

Mauna Loa on the island of Hawaii has gently sloping sides.

Sometimes, the lava is thin and runs downhill very fast. As it hardens, it builds a wider mountain with gentler slopes.

Volcanoes in the Sea

Many volcanoes rise up from the bottom of the ocean. Each time they **erupt**, they grow a little higher, until their **peaks** make islands.

This island is in Alaska. It is the top of a volcano in the ocean.

Sometimes a line of volcanoes grows above the surface of the ocean. Their peaks make a long line of islands.

A long, curving line of islands is called an island arc.

Different Eruptions

Volcanoes that **erupt** regularly are called **active** volcanoes. Some of these erupt gently. The **lava** seeps out quietly and the **gas** comes out in puffs.

This volcano is Mauna Loa in Hawaii. It is erupting quietly.

Mount St. Helens erupted violently in 1980.

Other volcanoes erupt like a bomb going off. Sometimes, a part of the mountain may be destroyed. Part of the **cone** of Mount St. Helens in Washington State was blown away.

The Power of Volcanoes

Volcanoes have a sudden and deadly power. The hot **lava** can destroy towns and kill people. The **ash** from the volcano can crush houses and plants.

Ash from this volcano has buried these houses.

This stream of hot lava is flowing over a road. Nothing can stop it.

When lava pours out of a volcano, it burns everything in its path. It flattens trees and plants, and covers the land.

Using Volcanoes

These fields lie next to a volcano in Spain.

Volcanoes can be useful. The **ash** and **lava** make the soil very good for farming. **Crops** grow well on the slopes.

The rocks near volcanoes are very hot. Power stations can use them to heat water. Steam from the hot water helps make **electricity** for factories and homes.

The steam made from the water helps to drive machines.

Studying Volcanoes

Scientists who study volcanoes are called **volcanologists**. They measure volcanoes and check for movements in the ground.

This volcanologist measures how far and fast the **lava** moves.

Scientists work in this **observatory** on a volcano. It is in Hawaii.

Scientists learn lots of things from studying volcanoes. They use the results to try to predict when a volcano will next **erupt**. This could save many people's lives.

Old Volcanoes

Volcanoes that have not **erupted** for many years are called **dormant** volcanoes. We sometimes say they are sleeping.

Mount Kilimanjaro in Tanzania, Africa, is a dormant volcano.

The sides of this volcano have been worn away by wind and rain.

Volcanoes that will never erupt again are called **extinct** volcanoes. Their **cones** are slowly worn down by the weather.

Volcano Map 1

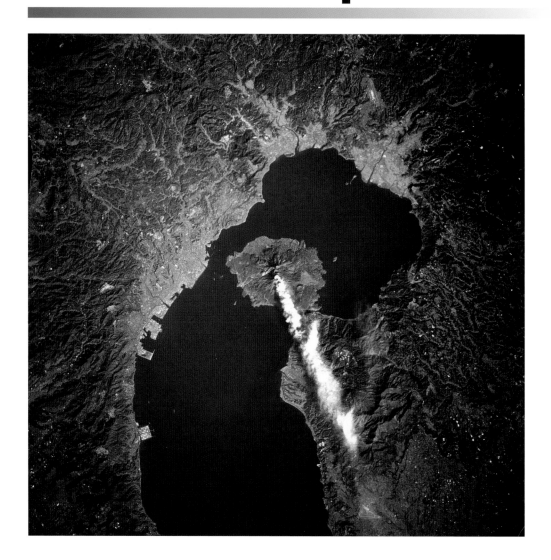

This is a photo of a volcano. It was taken by a **satellite** high above the earth. The volcano is an island close to the land. It is surrounded by water.

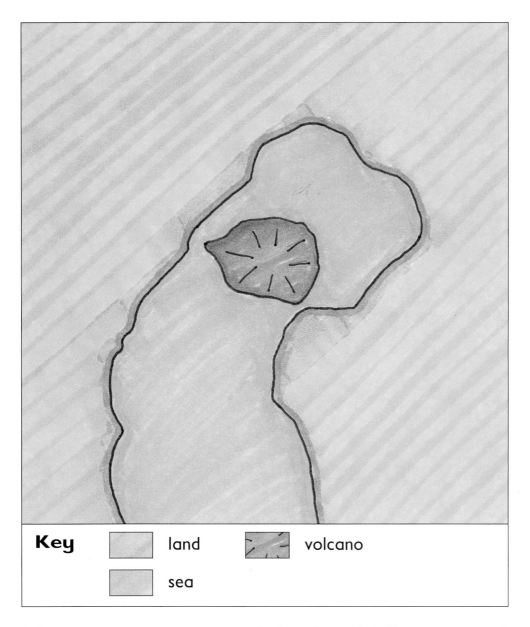

Key □ land ▨ volcano
□ sea

Maps are pictures of the land. This map shows us the same place as the photo. The key tells us what each color means. The blue color shows the water. The brown color shows the land.

Volcano Map 2

This photo shows a smaller part of the land, but you can see it more clearly. The volcano looks bigger. You can see a cloud of **ash** coming out of it. You can see a city at the edge of the land.

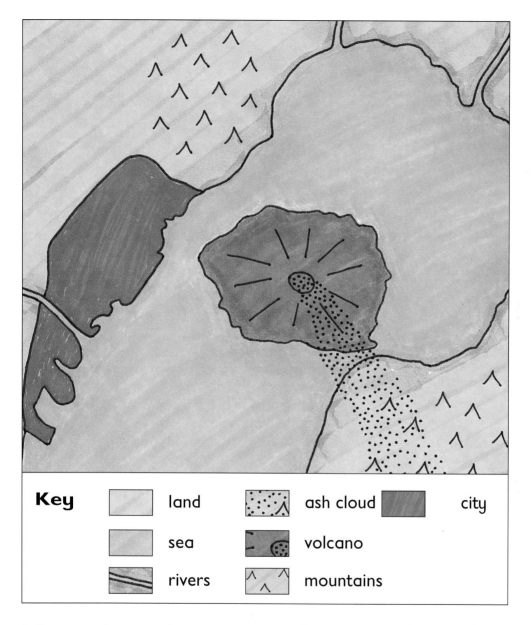

Key

land	ash cloud
sea	volcano
rivers	mountains
	city

The v-shaped points on this map show that some of the land is very high above the water. The red color shows the buildings in the city. The black dots show ash coming out of the volcano.

Volcano Map 3

This photo shows another volcano. It was taken from an airplane. It does not show the whole volcano, but you can see inside the **crater** very clearly.

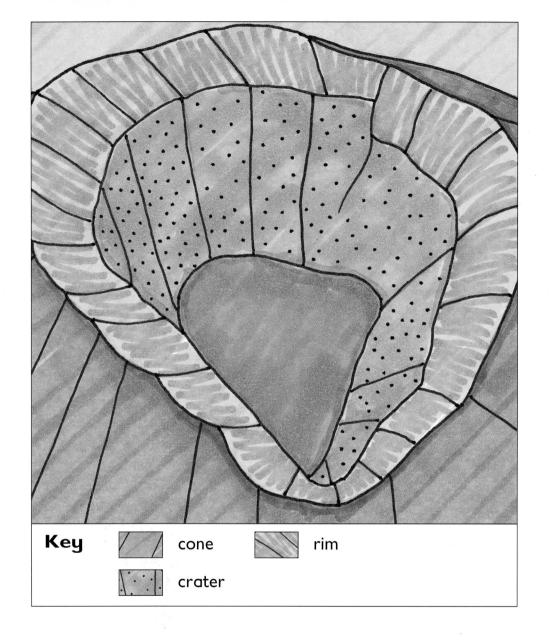

Key
/ cone
/ rim (hatched)
. crater (dotted)

The sides of the volcano are very steep. At the **rim** of the crater, the land sinks down steeply to the middle. The map shows the steep slopes of the **cone** with thin black lines.

Amazing Volcano Facts

About two thousand years ago, Mount Vesuvius in Italy suddenly **erupted**. The Roman town of Pompeii was buried in **ash.** This is part of the town.

Mauna Kea, on an island in Hawaii, is the
top of an underwater volcano. If you
measure it from the bottom of the ocean to
its **peak**, it is even taller than Mount Everest!

Glossary

active able to erupt

ash flakes and powder made by something that is burned

cone sides of a volcano

crater large round opening at the top of a volcano

crop plants a farmer grows in fields, such as corn

dormant has not erupted for many years

electricity power that makes appliances such as lights, televisions, and radios, work

erupt to suddenly shoot out **lava** and ash

extinct will never erupt again

gas something that is not water or air, and that gets bigger to fill the space around it

lava hot, liquid rock that shoots out of a volcano from inside the Earth

observatory special building where people like scientists can watch a volcano and make measurements

peak top of a hill or mountain

rim edge around something round

satellite special machine that goes around the Earth in space. It can take photographs of the Earth.

volcanologist person who studies volcanoes

More Books to Read

Herman, Gail. *The Magic School Bus Blows Its Top: A Book about Volcanoes.* New York: Scholastic, 1996.

Mainard, Christopher. *Why Do Volcanoes Erupt?.* New York: D K Publishing, Incorporated, 1997.

Murray, Peter. *Volcanoes.* Chanhassen, Minn.: The Child's World, Incorporated, 1995. An older reader can help you with this book.

Owen, Andy, and Miranda Ashwell. *Mountains.* Des Plaines, Ill.: Heinemann, 1998

Index